18 JAZZ DUETS FOR TWO TRUMPETS

T0085277

To access audio visit:
www.halleonard.com/mylibrary

Enter Code
4137-2275-7786-9258

ISBN 978-1-59615-735-4

Music Minus One

EXCLUSIVELY DISTRIBUTED BY

HAL•LEONARD®

7777 W. BLUEMOUND RD. P.O. BOX 13819 MILWAUKEE, WI 53213

Visit Hal Leonard Online at
www.halleonard.com

CONTENTS

1. Just For Swinging

2. A Swinger

4 bar bass & drum intro.

3. A Study in Fragmentation

2 bar drum intro.

4. Chinatown After Hours

2 bar drum intro.

5. For Lovers

2 bar bass & drum intro.

6. Gypsy

2 bar bass & drum intro.

7. Riff Time

1 ¾ bar drum intro.

8. G Swing

2 bar drum intro.

9. Dirty, Low Down Blues

1 ½ bar & drum intro.

10. More Big Band

2 bar bass & drum intro.

11. Pretty Music

2 bar bass & drum intro.

12. Fun With Chord Progressions

2 bar drum intro.

13. Very Fast, Light, Basie Touch

4 bar drum intro.

14. For Sheep Herders Only

3 ¹/₃ bars bass intro.

15. Chamber Music 1968

2 bar drum intro.

16. Music To Get Your Jollies By

2 bar drum intro.

17. Torchy

2 bar drum intro.

18. Drawing Room Music With A Beat

2 bar drum intro.

Engraving: Wieslaw Novak

MORE GREAT BRASS PUBLICATIONS FROM
Music Minus One

CLASSICAL PUBLICATIONS

J.S. Bach –
Two-Part Inventions & Other Masterworks for Two Trumpets
Trumpet Edition
Performed by Robert Zottola
Book/Online Audio
00124386 ....$19.99

W.A. Mozart –
Horn Concertos
No. 2 in E-Flat Major, KV 417
No. 3 in E-Flat Major, KV 447
French Horn Edition
Performed by Willard Zirk
Accompaniment: Stuttgart Festival Orchestra
Book/Online Audio
00400388 ....$22.99

Igor Stravinsky –
L'Histoire du Soldat
Performed by Gerald Kocher, trumpet; Sean Mahoney, trombone
Accompaniment: Parnassus
Book/Online Audio
00400442 **Trumpet**.......$19.99

Advanced
Trombone Solos
Accompaniment: Harriet Wingreen, piano
Book/Online Audio
00400694 **Volume 1**.....$16.99
Book/CD Packs
00400149 **Volume 2** $14.99
00400738 **Volume 3** $14.99
00400739 **Volume 4** $14.99
~~vn~~loadable Edition
~~0~~07390 **Volume 5**........................$14.99

Intermediate
French Horn Solos
Performed by Dale Clevenger
Downloadable Editions
01007043 **Volume 1**......$14.99
01007325 **Volume 2**......$14.99
01007327 **Volume 3**......$14.99
Book/CD Pack
00400395 **Volume 4**......$14.99

JAZZ/STANDARDS

20 Dixieland
Classics
Trumpet Edition
Performed by John Hoffman
Accompaniment: The Dixieland All-Stars
Book/Online Audio
00400617 ....$16.99

Play the Music of
Burt Bacharach
Performed by the Jack Six All-Star Orchestra
Book/Online Audio
00400647 **Trumpet**.......$16.99
Book/CD Pack
00400651 **Trombone**....$14.99

Classic Ballads
for Trombone
Trombone Edition
Performed by Ira Nepus
Book/Online Audio
00131620 ....$16.99

From Dixie to Swing
No. 1 in D Major, No. 2 in A Minor, No. 3 in G Minor
Performed by Dick Wellstood All-Stars
Book/Online Audio
00400619 **Trumpet**..........$16.99
Book/CD Pack
00400622 **Trombone**.......$14.99

The Isle of Orleans
Performed by Tim Laughlin's New Orleans All-Stars
Book/2-CD Packs
00400446 **Trumpet**.......$14.99
00400461 **Trombone**....$14.99

New Orleans Classics
The Chicago & New York Jazz Scene
Performed by Tim Laughlin's New Orleans All-Stars
Book/Online Audio
00400025 **Trumpet**.......$19.99
Book/2-CD Pack
00400026 **Trombone** $19.99

Music for Brass
Ensemble
Performed by Tim Laughlin's New Orleans All-Stars
Book/CD Packs
00400432 **Trumpet**.......$14.99
00400451 **Trombone**....$14.99
00400519 **Tuba** $14.99
Downloadable Edition
01007040 **French Horn**.$14.99

Play Ballads
with a Band
Performed by the Bob Wilber All-Star Band
Book/CD Packs
00400645 **Trumpet**.......$14.99
Book/Online Audio
00400649 **Trombone**....$16.99

Signature Series
Trumpet Editions
Performed by Bob Zottola
Book/Online Audio
00138903 **Volume 1**.....$16.99
Book/CD Packs
00142697 **Volume 2**.....$14.99
00147464 **Volume 3**.....$14.99

Swing with a Band
Performed by Steve Patrick, trumpet; Roy Agee, trombone
Book/CD Pack
00400650 **Trombone**....$14.99

To see a full listing of
Music Minus One publications, visit
halleonard.com/MusicMinusOne

Music Minus One
HAL•LEONARD®
Prices, contents, and availability subject
to change without notice.